Power,
Passion,
Honor
& Glory
Five Heroes of
Modern Golf

Power,
Passion,
Honor
& Glory

Five Heroes of
Modern Golf

Photographs by Gerald Sprayregen
Text by William Hallberg

With a foreword by James Dodson
Design by Vicki Sylvester

This 1999 edition is published by

SPORTS-POETRY IN MOTION

10 Southeastern Farms Road

Pound Ridge, New York 10576

914/234-2618

email: http://www.gsprayregen@compuserve.com

Printed and bound in the United States by R.R. Donnelly & Sons Co.

Power, Passion, Honor & Glory is not a publication authorized by Arnold Palmer, Jack Nicklaus, Tom Watson,
Greg Norman, Tiger Woods, the PGA, or their representatives or related enterprises.

ISBN 0-19671933-0-3

Library of Congress Catalog Card Number: 99-075730

1 2 3 4 5 6 7 8 9 10 03 02 01 00 99

This book is dedicated to my three children, Nicholas, Lisa and Pamela. Ever since they were born, they have been at the center of my life and my thoughts. They have had the blessings of my parents, as part of their heritage, and Fredrica, as their mother. Therefore, if they had a slightly eccentric father, they were strong enough to cope. Each of them has become a good person with solid values and is in the midst of raising a wonderful family. I am proud to be their father. — BBD

Our sincere appreciation to the following individuals and organizations: Joel Teig; David Wilkes and his crew at LPC; Julieanne Kost at Adobe; Chuck De Luca at Nikon Electronic Imaging; Judy George; Mel Cowher at R. R. Donnelley & Sons; Dominic Callan, *Schwing Magazine;* George Peper, *Golf Magazine;* Gerry Yohcum and Robert Musich at Rockrimmon Country Club; Michael Murphy; Mark Serota; Rick Oleshak; Rick Wester; Brooks Johnson; Gillian Ashley, our wonderful editor; James Dodson; Bill Hallberg for his wonderful writing and for all of his efforts above and beyond...and to Frances Sprayregen for her love of the game.

Our very special thanks to Robert Carney who has become our unofficial advisor on this book, and whose caring and sage suggestions have helped us immeasurably. Bob's enthusiasm for this project has been very meaningful to us.

Grateful acknowledgement is given to the following people for a number of short quotes in this book: *Jack Nicklaus, My Story,* with Ken Bowden; *Stalking the Shark,* Carl Vieland; *The Shark,* Lauren St. John; *Getting Back to Basics,* Tom Watson; *Playing Through,* Earl Woods; *Tiger Woods,* Tim Rosaforte; David Leadbetter, Lee Trevino, Peter Jacobsen, Arnold Palmer, Jack Nicklaus, Tom Watson, Greg Norman, and Tiger Woods.

Contents

Introduction

Except for a few rounds played with my twin brother and my mother, my relationship with golf used to be platonic at best. The game was too staid, too mysterious, and too frustrating. Basketball, tennis and baseball were my sports. Only recently have I become more intimately involved with golf, in a way I could never have imagined, even though I rarely play the game. Instead, I create images!

After having photographed myriad sporting events from bullfighting to bicycle racing to yachting to NBA basketball, I inevitably followed the likes of Nicklaus, Palmer, and Woods as they performed a kind of magic that seemed alien to a total hacker like myself. Maybe I was drawn, too, by the strange requirements of the game: after all, a golfer is expected to clobber a tiny orb great distances, with the goal of nudging the ball deftly across a slick green carpet towards an impossibly small cup. How, I wondered, could anyone develop a passion for such a queer sport as this? However, the more time I spent lugging my equipment around the world's fairways, the more I appreciated the subtle artistry of this greenest of all sports. I learned that every shot is different in golf. The terrain varies from moment to moment, as do the playing conditions. Even the competitive circumstances are wildly influential on how the game is played. Perhaps there was something to this game after all. Anyway, I have developed a unique brand of love for golf, a sort of voyeuristic obsession, one might say; instead of woods and irons, the tools of my trade are cameras, lenses, monopods and filters.

Three years ago when my partner Vicki Sylvester and I decided to produce our first golf book, I spent day after day in various libraries poring through anything written on the subject of golf, in my desire to try to understand the all-consuming passion that infiltrates the minds and souls of golfers. I read over seventy golf books written by the best practitioners of the genre: Updike, Murphy, Dodson, Bamberger...and, of course, William Hallberg, one of the collaborators responsible for the book you now hold in your hands. My goal in enlisting the talents of Bill and Vicki was to create the most beautiful golf book of all time. Perhaps our combined efforts have at least come close to achieving that end.

Being a professional golfer is hard work. This is a concept I can identify with, as shooting the touring pros is an equally arduous undertaking. When a sports photographer shoots a baseball game or a basketball game, or even a tennis match, most of the time you see him sitting on his duff for three hours, joshing with his compatriots, snapping an image when the occasion demands it. Not so in golf, where I averaged twelve hours per day shooting golf tournaments. Many pros arrived at the golf course just before the sun rose on the fairways. I tried to be there before they are. When the day's play was finished, they frequented the practice green and the driving range, correcting those flaws that undid them, or building on their virtues. In between dawn and dusk, I usually walked thirty-six holes with two cameras around my neck, another on a monopod, carrying five lenses (one as long as your arm) and forty to fifty rolls of film. I dangled from scaffolding, climbed trees, hid behind tents, jostled amongst the masses, all to get that one great photograph. To sustain me, I carried an apple and a bottle of water. Golf is a warm-weather sport, and often the sun was pummeling down on me, or else the buffeting rains were giving me a good soaking. I endured tempests at Pebble Beach, windstorms in Vegas, sizzling heat in Orlando, and every other species of meteorological assault in order to get the pictures of the game's greatest players, who are the subjects of this book.

Our criteria for selecting our superstars was simple: they had to dominate the world of golf in their prime, and they have to be currently active in either the PGA or Senior Tours. Only five heroes emerged. Thus, brilliant players like Gary Player and Lee Trevino, Nick Faldo and Nick Price are not included, simply because they had the misfortune to be playing during the reigns of golf's monarchs. Arnold Palmer was the King of the Tour during the late 50s and early 60s. His sixty Tour victories have been surpassed by only three other golfers (Snead, 81; Nicklaus, 70; Hogan, 63). Arnie has seven Majors to his credit and has earned the PGA Lifetime Achievement Award. Then along came the Bear, Jack Nicklaus, who was considered by many to be the greatest player in the history of the game. From 1964 to 1976, Jack dominated the PGA Tour, and in 1988 was named Golfer of the Century by *Golf Magazine*. His most stunning achievements were eighteen professional championships in the Majors, more than any other golfer. He also had nineteen second-place finishes. The next star wasTom Watson, who had the wisdom to be born a decade after Nicklaus. Starting in 1977, he ruled the fairways for seven years, securing twenty-nine victories during that time on the Tour. During this stretch he had six consecutive years of winning at least three tournaments per year. He is the holder of eight Major championships. Then from 1986 to 1995 Greg Norman was the man to beat in any tournament he entered—although he too frequently beat himself! He won eighteen Tour victories as well as fifty-six international championships. He also has two British Open victories to his credit and was runner-up eight other times. And finally, the incomparable Tiger

Woods arrived on the scene, possessing impossible skills and a kind of glamor that lifted golf to the front page of the sports section of the daily newspaper. In the history of the world, there may well have been more words written about Tiger Woods than any other twenty-three-year-old. Can this be justified? The evidence suggests that it is. Tiger has been hailed as potentially the greatest golfer to play the game, and surely the most talented. In the years 1991 through 1996 he dominated the U.S. Junior Amateur Championships and the U.S. Amateur Championships. In 1994, *Golf World* named him Man of the Year. In 1997 he won his first Masters and was named Male Athlete of the Year by the Associated Press (he was the first golfer to be so honored in twenty-six years). In 1999 he won his second Major, the PGA Championship. In the first eight months of 1999 he has had five victories on the Tour, and his accumulated earnings are $4.27 million, surpassing all previous Tour records. Tiger promises to energize the game, as Palmer did before him, and pave the way for heroes of the new millenium. I envy the photographers, who will bear witness to these events and record for prosterity those thrilling moments.

My fascination for golf has evolved from platonic to passionate over the years. Every worthwhile love affair hinges on crystalline moments that capture the essence of the relationship. These photographs, accompanied by William Hallberg's words, provide an artistic document of moments with which we can all identify. Vicki, Bill and I hope that *Power, Passion, Honor & Glory* will feed your affection for the game while capturing its undeniable romance.

—*Gerald Sprayregen*

Foreword

For a while when I was a little kid, I genuinely thought Arnold Daniel Palmer invented the game of golf. That's because every time I saw golf on television or read about it in magazines or newspapers, Arnold Palmer's name was always mentioned with almost breathless awe and admiration. It was 1960, the height of Arnie mania, weeks after his miraculous finish at Cherry Hills enabled him to capture his one and only U.S. Open Championship. I was seven years old and deeply impressed that people hailed Palmer the "KIng of Golf."

Like millions of fellow babyboomers, Arnie's rise was my Ground Zero in the game. To our unformed and uninitiated golf brains, it was inconceivable that anything great—or anyone as wonderful—could have happened in golf before Arnie came along with his youthful charisma and swashbuckling style of play, hitching his pants and smiling warmly at his army.

Imagine my surprise when my father informed me *his* golf hero, Slammin' Sam Snead, had also set the golf world on fire and been the greatest player of his day ten years before Palmer. And before Snead, he further explained, Ben Hogan and Byron Nelson respectively climbed to the summit of the game, while before them Walter Hagen had become the first genuine world superstar in the professional ranks of golf. Perhaps the greatest player of them all, he finally essayed, preceded the great Hagen—the great amateur Bobby Jones.

Dad's intent was not to diminish the coming of Arnie The King—but, rather, simply to show me, a knee-high hacking neophyte, that golf was much bigger than one man: it was a game extremely deep in sporting tradition, with a pedigreed evolution of playing stars that were not only the unchallenged golf champions of their days, but also distinctly, and almost mysteriously, perfect for their particular *moments* in time. In the golden age of amateur golf, for instance, Bob Jones's heroic Grand Slam unquestionably set the stage for Hagen's evolutionary showmanship and pomaded brilliance as the game's first true touring professional, which in turn inspired young working-class blokes named Nelson, Hogan and Snead to abandon club jobs and strike out for riches on the nascent professional circuit, which in time convinced a former Coast Guardie-turned-Cleveland-paint-salesman named Palmer to take a shot at immortality in professional golf. Bob begat Walter who begat Sam...and so forth.

That's the gospel of golf I grew up reading, at any rate, and in the nearly forty years I've been lucky enough to be around the game both as man and boy, spectator and journalist, that point has been driven home again and again—every four or five years, it seems, with the sudden nova-like explosion of a new dazzling young superstar in the game.

To update the lineage theory a bit, the conventional view is that Arnie's unprecedented fame and drawing power (it's been estimated he attracted more than 20 million people to the game) established a benchmark nobody could ever challenge—until a rawly barbered, pudgily muscular, stolid-faced "bear" of a kid named Nicklaus came out of Ohio with a sweeping powerfade to knock the King off his throne. Watching from the wings, a brainy Stanford psychology graduate named Tommy Watson quietly waited for his moment and honed his short game to lethal expertise until, seven or eight years along, he outdueled the Golden Bear at Turnberry in 1977—the greatest final day in British Open history—to capture the second of his five Claret Jugs and place his own imprimatur on golf immortality.

Meanwhile, half a world away, a blond-haired Aussie kid who looked more like a surfer than a golf prodigy suddenly came of age, having worn out the copy of Nickluas's *Golf My Way* given to him one Christmas by his mother, and played his way as tenaciously as a great white shark to the PGA Tour from the beaches Down Under. Right on cue, according to this armchair theory of golf evolution, Greg Norman won his first PGA Tour tournament the year after Watson won his last British Open, announcing the birth of the game's latest charismatic phenom, the first truly international golf star since Gary Player.

In a sense, all four of these modern heroes of the game contributed to the wondrous creation of Elderick "Tiger" Woods, whose three consecutive National Amateur Championships presented us the most auspicious professional debut in the history of the game. Given the pedigree, it's probably no surprise that Tiger hasn't disappointed—and if you look closely, you'll see traces of the others in his seemingly flawless game. Palmer's power and fire-in-the-belly passion; the unearthly Nicklaus concentration and ballstriking prowess; the magical putting touch of Tom Watson in his prime; Norman's elegant natural magnetism. In a sense, here on the cusp of the Millenium, Tiger Woods is the apotheosis of golf in the 20th Century—The Golf Century.

In this delightful collection of animated photographs of the five most influential players of the modern game, framed and enhanced by Bill Hallberg's nimble and evocative prose, photographer Gerry Sprayregen brilliantly captures the essence of their timeless attractions—the majesty of their swings as well as the magic of their personalities. Some of these living legends appear a bit older than we remember them or would prefer to think they've become on the fairways of Father Time, while others are at their peaks or just beginning the journey to golf immortality. It doesn't really matter—*all* of the individual elements that made these men such a joy and inspiration to be seen and savored and ultimately fondly remembered, are here. These beguiling pages will remind you why golf is a game of heroes, constantly evolving, always wearing a new and interesting face.

—*James Dodson*

Arnold Palmer

In 1959, early on a Saturday evening, while runoff from rooftop snowmelt splashed onto the bushes outside the window of our "faculty housing," I was watching Challenge Golf on television. It was a second-hand Motorola TV, already something of a relic, and the golfers were stretched into Gothic goons by an incurable defect in the dying picture tube. Thus, my first recollection of Arnold Palmer, paired with the lithesome Billy Casper against a foredoomed, albeit towering twosome, was that of an ungainly man approximately seven feet tall with simian arms and a long face full of pathos. Despite the obstacles to an accurate appreciation of the human, not to mention the geographical, dimensions of the contest, I was nevertheless drawn to Arnold Palmer. The vectors indicating the lengths and directions of his drives were clearly longer than those of his competitors, if slightly off course. He became a magical figure for me, one I was sure I knew as well as any soul on earth. I discerned his ups and downs, and I thrived or suffered according to his fortunes. He was my hero, my idol, my role model. I watched him week after week on Saturday evenings as he slashed drives down the alternately corpulent or emaciated fairways, gouged golf balls from their nests in the deep rough, and canned impossible putts to assure victory. Merely watching him traipse the California fairways while the Ohio sky loomed heavy with snow was the absolute palliative for the winter doldrums that dragged into the wet Midwestern spring. His heroic stature caught hold of my imagination and has not let go to this day.

When you are a legend like Arnold Palmer, it is inevitable that a kind of folklore trails behind you, reaching deep into the landscape of your personal history. Here in North Carolina, for example, anyone old enough to remember Arnie's stint at Wake Forest has a tale, often apocryphal, of those days when he was a Demon Deacon. I was playing golf the other day with an older gentleman not part of my regular golfing circle, who told me about a football game in 1948 when Arnold Palmer provided the halftime entertainment. As the story goes, someone had placed a deflated inner tube at midfield, and Arnie stood at the goal line with a bucket of golf balls. His task was to pitch as many balls as possible inside the target. Any success was greeted with wild applause; near misses evoked hyperbolic groans from the yellow-sweatered fans in the bleachers. Of course, Arnie's performance, as reported, defies plausibility. Could he really have landed even one ball inside that circular target from fifty yards away? Not likely, until one considers how Arnie's life, from the earliest days of his stardom, defied plausibility.

I invested my youth in Arnold Palmer. I imitated his mannerisms, affected a goofy, looping follow-through intended to replicate Arnie's, I developed my own version of the trademark cocking of the head, I puffed imaginary cigarettes and blew phantom smoke towards the summer sky. It was all a vast failure. Nobody was Arnie but Arnie himself. Those mannerisms—the impish grin, the quizzical squint, the thin-lipped laugh, the hitching of the trousers—so indelibly etched in my imagination—are perhaps more theatrical than earnest. The camera has always loved Arnie, whose idiosyncracies are as endearing as they are strange.

In 1960, Arnie won the Masters, and then, in dramatic fashion, the U.S. Open at Cherry Hills that summer, coming from seven shots back on the final nine holes to win the title. Then, in July of that same year, during the British Open, he came within a single stroke of matching the final score of Kel Nagle, who won the tournament. Arnie was all but invincible that year, and his face was on the cover of nearly every major national magazine. He was *Sports Illustrated's* Sportsman of the Year.

Gary Player once said of Arnie, "He's better out of the trees than he is out of the fairways. And, of course, that was, and is, so much of his appeal. Even now, he can pull off that miracle shot, from 100 yards out, that finds its way from no man's land to the cup."

"What other people may find in poetry or art museums, I find in the flight of a good drive."

Arnold Palmer

Perhaps the quintessential story of Palmer's devotion to his fans unfolded several decades ago at the height of his popularity, in the midst of a series of exhibitions held in Australia and New Zealand. There was Arnie, asleep in is Hobart Hotel room, clad in his skivvies, when the fire alarm sounded, chasing him and several dozen Japanese businessmen from their rooms. While the Japanese, due to an early flight out, were able to exit the building fully dressed, suitcases in hand, Arnie could only grab a sheet to wrap around himself.

Imagine the King standing on the pre-dawn street, half a continent from home, hair roostered up, half-naked, listening to the alarm's piercing wail. Then he was recognized. *"Palmer-san, Palmer-san,"* the fellow evacuees shouted. Soon Arnie was signing autographs, which he continued to do until well after the siren fell silent.

No golfer before or since Palmer's prime has been so known for the way he moves a club head through space. Even now, in the fragile twilight of a long career, the swing is the emblem that most clearly defines him. There are other emblems, of course, with which we are universally familiar. But the essence of Arnold Palmer is that impossible swing, violent and flamboyant. The follow-through isn't really a follow-through at all, as much as a fishtail skid-out on the heels of that car wreck of a golf swing.

I had every reason to welcome Jack Nicklaus when he thundered onto the scene like a golden steamroller at that 1960 Masters tournament, which he lost to Arnold Palmer by only two shots, and only because my hero made incredible birdies on the last two holes. Jack was from Columbus, just down the road, a fellow Buckeye, a college boy, a gentleman, a prodigy. I didn't hate him, but I politely rooted against him. Jack's drives, while monstrous, stayed in the fairway, and the rest of his game was calculated and under control. He played a high fade; Arnie ripped a low draw.

Jack was genial but slightly enigmatic and even a little bit uncomfortable before the camera. His voice was incongruously high-pitched in contrast to Arnie's pleasant baritone. Arnie was whimsical; Jack was serious. But mostly, it came down to my loving Arnie because I was a kid capable of embracing only one hero at a time; the heir apparent had arrived to threaten the King. Jack, not the least bit intimidated by Arnie's magic, plodded brilliantly along week after week, playing his own game, analyzing the golf courses with intelligence, yet never quite relating to a generation of fans who had been brought to the game by a blue collar everyman of undeniable charisma. Now that the two giants have found their own niches in the pantheon of golf, their fondness and admiration for one another are evident whenever they appear together at charity events and the occasional senior tournament.

A rnie had more triumphs to come, but as early as 1962 the torch was slipping from Arnie's grasp and into the clutches of Jack Nicklaus, a man for whom adulation would be hard-earned. It's possible that Arnie felt more intimidated by Jack than Jack did in the presence of Arnie. And Jack was still an amateur. Throughout their careers, the two arch-rivals have held each other in the highest regard. Perhaps, deep down, Arnie envies Jack's unapproachable record and his long career. And Jack may be secretly jealous of the love and affection bestowed upon his adversary. But they have always honored one another for what each has brought to the game they both love. They have their respective sports equipment businesses, they have each designed dozens of renowned golf courses, and of course they still compete—but always as respectful gentlemen. They play in charity events together, and Skins Games, but these are companionabe adventures by definition. Between the first tee and the eighteenth green of a major golf tournament, they are benign competitors.

Arnie and Jack have helped to define one another, and the game itself, and there is still a strong suggestion that there's something left to accomplish on the golf course.

"There is a philosophy of boldness—to take

advantage of every tiny opening towards victory."

Arnold Palmer

Arnold Palmer helped fundamentally change the game of golf. He has a belly now, and decades of sun have furrowed the skin at the back of his neck. His hide is as leathery as an old lion's, his health has faltered and rebounded of late, and he moves with slightly less grace up the nation's fairways. While the Palmer of old exuded raw power, the older Palmer seems a more stately figure, grand and immovable like a monument to his glory days.

What most fans failed to realize was that Palmer was one of the great putters of all time. Bobbie Jones once said, *"If I ever needed an eight-foot putt and everything I owned depended on it, I would want Arnold Palmer to putt it for me."*

Arnie ruled the golfing scene at a time before the advent of the omnipresent coaches who are paid vast sums to tweak and fine-tune the takeaways, the downswings and follow-throughs of a new crop of lions. Purses for many of today's tournaments exceed the total earnings of most of the greatest professionals of the '50s and '60s. Arnie, like his contemporaries, was essentially self-taught. He was the son of a hard-working club pro in Latrobe, Pennsylvania, who instructed him in the basics, but perhaps not much more than that. As Arnie has stated, *"Pop didn't teach me golf, he taught me discipline."* Among touring professionals in the early '50s and '60s, there were plenty of peculiar, even insanely illogical, swings to be seen. Arnie's friend Doug Ford, as the joke goes, could execute his swing within the confines of a phone booth. Bob Rosberg grasped the club like a baseball bat. Miller Barber obviously concocted his neo-Baroque golf swing while killing time in eighth-grade study hall.

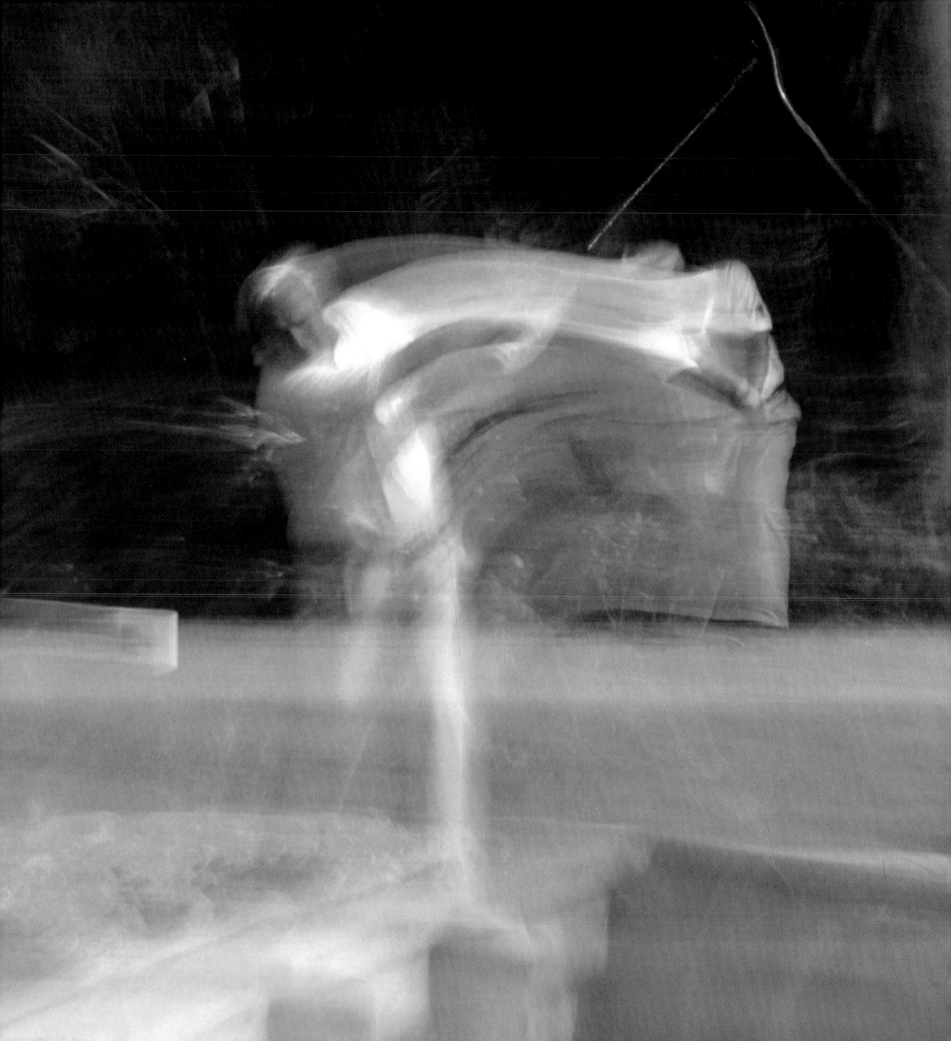

And the fact is that even in his heyday, the ball often traveled into terrae incognitae—waste high grass, gloomy clumps of impenetrable trees, parking lots and picnic baskets. No one could say for sure where Palmer's ball would land, and the uncertainty made his game a drama. And the excitement came from the swing.

Nobody has a swing with the pure theatricality of Arnold Palmer's. He's part swashbuckler, part samurai, and part Lord High Executioner—with a bit of wheat thresher thrown in. One could hardly imagine a predictable outcome deriving from such a wicked flail.

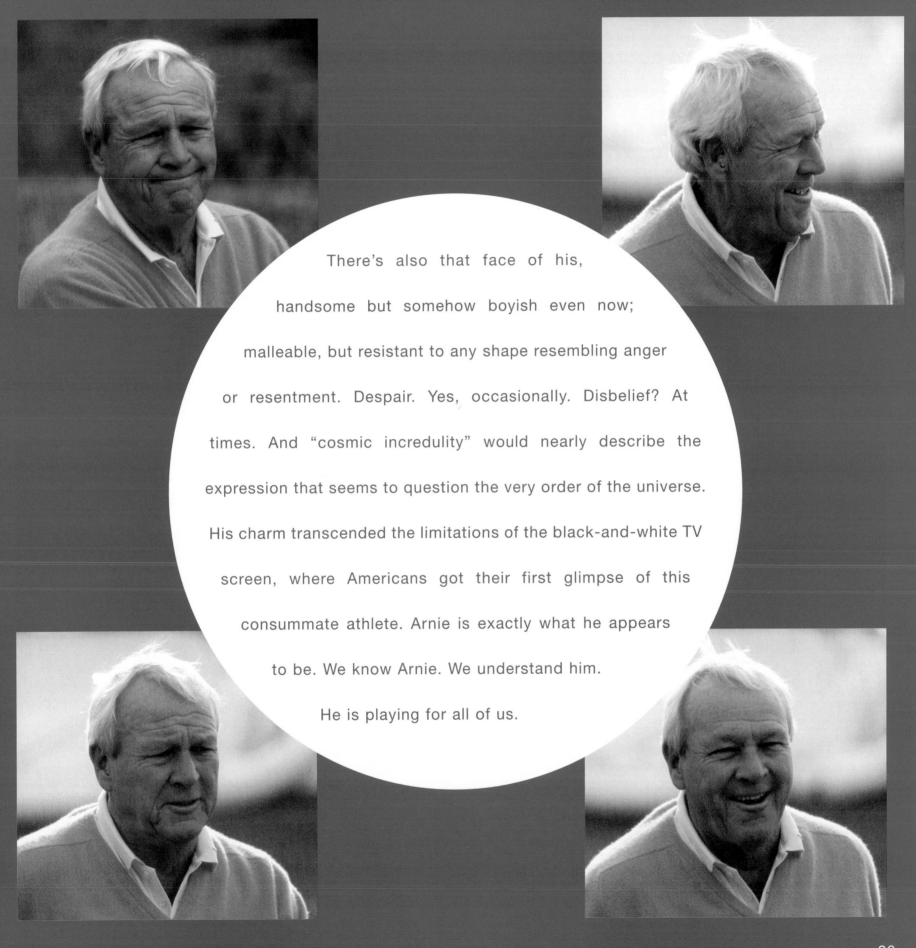

There's also that face of his, handsome but somehow boyish even now; malleable, but resistant to any shape resembling anger or resentment. Despair. Yes, occasionally. Disbelief? At times. And "cosmic incredulity" would nearly describe the expression that seems to question the very order of the universe. His charm transcended the limitations of the black-and-white TV screen, where Americans got their first glimpse of this consummate athlete. Arnie is exactly what he appears to be. We know Arnie. We understand him.

He is playing for all of us.

In April of 1999, when Arnie waved good-bye to Augusta after having missed the cut, I felt suddenly older, even a little bit diminished by the knowledge that my boyhood hero would no longer saunter amongst the azaleas at Amen Corner. Watching him cross the granite bridge for the last time, then brave four more brutal golf holes and finally march up the steep 18th fairway into the embrace of the assembled multitude, I could feel the sun setting on the last traces of my youth. I sensed the arrival of uncompromising adulthood, probably a good thing for a middle-aged man like me, but a painful concession nonetheless. After all, doesn't golf make youths of us all? The answer is surely yes. Even so, such farewells as Arnie's to Augusta mark a turning point for boomers like me as much as for him, with whom we have identified for so many decades.

I wonder what echoes rang in his ears as he strode those last yards to the final hole. He could no longer say to himself, "Wait until next year." There would be no next year. Did he memorize the smell of the fairways, the faint scent of the concession stand, the cheers, the brush of wind across his forehead? How did it feel to know that age had finally overtaken him, and had done so in full public view?

When two heroic figures like Palmer and Michael Jordan combine forces at charity events, the gate receipts are sufficient to rebuild a small city; meanwhile, MJ and the King have a hell of a good time making it all happen. As members of a very small fraternity of living sports legends, they share an arena where the glare of publicity can be intense, which might explain the obvious joy they derive from each other's company. *"Let's see if you can catch up to that one,"* Michael says after booming a nice one down the fairway. Arnie says, *"That was a seven wood, right?"* MJ just shakes his head and smiles.

Now he is a veteran, tawny and a little tired. His role is more ceremonial, ambassadorial, than it is competitive. He lends his name to this cause, that event, an occasional Skins Game, a new charity. His golf apparel company is worth millions, and his endorsement contracts alone have made him fabulously wealthy. He plays a good game still, but not a great one. His hair is white, what there is of it, and the lines are deeper in his face. He slathers his skin with sunscreen, eats sensible foods, signs autographs and chats with his adoring fans.

Whether he's playing in a fundraiser or a major tournament, Arnie pauses mid-fairway—or even mid-green—if a plane zooms overhead. He gazes skyward toward the source of the engine noise as if his mind is really elsewhere. He is flawlessly up to date on the latest aircraft, such is his passion for flight. He pilots his own jet, and has done so for decades now. It's a curious juxtaposition: the turf is firm and green underfoot; the sky is vast and blue and eternal. A golfer, if he is to be successful, commands the ground on which he walks and the air through which his shots fly. Arnie, perhaps more than any golfer, commands both elements.

Arnie, by his own admission, still wants to win. His army has dissipated but it has not deserted. The champion in him will not relinquish the hope; he still believes one great stretch awaits him, wherein perhaps the steeple clocks in St. Andrews, or the famous Inverness clock in Toledo, will stop its inexorable progress in deference to him, and come to life only to ring its bells in honor of his miraculous triumph over time itself. Yet deep inside he knows, as Whitman said, *"Time avails not. It waits for no man. It makes beggars of us all."* If, however, one golfer in this century can make time stand still, that man is Arnold Palmer.

Jack Nicklaus

On a Sunday afternoon early in April 1986, I was sitting in an Irish pub in Chicago with a long-lost friend and golfing buddy who chanced to have attended the same academic conference as I, right there in the Windy City. During the ordeal, Jack Nicklaus's adventures at the Masters were not in the forefront of our thoughts, so much as escaping at last the dreary weight of academe. However, after the last flatulent scholarly paper had been presented, and the conference was blessedly over (obviously, the legendary Chicago winds were generated at the podium in the Drake Hotel Ballroom), our minds turned to golf. We both had flights to catch later on, but, for the sake of auld lang syne, we decided to wile away our remaining hours together drinking draught Old Style Beer and watching a few holes of the Masters at a pub with a blinking neon Shamrock in the front window. Little did we know when we took our seats at the dusky bar beneath a 36-inch TV screen that the Golden Bear would change all of our plans. What unfolded on that spring day in Augusta was so dramatic, so spectacular and so emotional that we were willing to miss our flights home and trust the vagaries of fate, just so we could see the event through to its amazing climax.

There it was, vivid before us on the TV screen: the Nicklaus magic was flowing once again...into the grooves of his irons...into the blade of his cartoonishly macrocephalic putter. (Calmed by the music of Whitney Houston, wafting from an open window somewhere beyond the trees) he began making birdies at Amen Corner, then at 15 and 16. He chased after his putts as they rolled toward the cup, raised his fists in triumph, smiled the old Nicklaus smile. The crowd's cheers were so voluminous that even the sleepy drunks in the pub awakened to see what on earth was happening. It was Nicklaus, of course, striding jubilantly up the last fairway amidst tumultuous cheers. Jack claims that his eyes were so full of tears as he marched up the hill that he could hardly see the ball waiting for him on the green. I was nearly as choked up as Jack, and so were the bar patrons, all of whom were now glued to the TV screen.

It was truly a heroic moment, probably the most memorable image of my golf-mad life. After tapping in his final putt, Jack sat in the Eisenhower Cottage to see how things would unfold. But the outcome was meant to be; we all knew it. Greg Norman, forever cursed, followed the preordained script by pushing a four-iron approach into the bleachers at 18, and Seve, of course, had already found water at number 15. Fate had seemingly determined that The Bear should triumph one more time, and I wasn't about to miss out on the festivities, nor was my pal Jim. Norman holed out perfunctorily, one shot back, and the tournament was decided. Jim and I high-fived and hooted and toasted the golfing gods who rule the fairways and greens. We were not alone in our joy. We middle-aged semi-inebriates felt suddenly immortal, as if time had stood still. Jack was still the hero he had always been.

Now the Bear is almost sixty. When Jack was ten, his dad, on doctor's orders, took up the game of golf to rehabilitate an injured heel. His son tagged along and was allowed to play a hole or two from time to time. Within a year, the child was father to the man, at least on the golf course. Half a century later, Jack has a paunch, his hair is thinning, his eyesight is failing, and he has a new space-age hip to replace his crumbling original. He rarely plays the Senior Tour, which, in his mind, perhaps, seems altogether too ceremonial, like a sentimental showcase for oldsters who can't cut it on the junior circuit. Jack's corpuscles still percolate during the major tournaments when he can compete with the best golfers in the world. *"When I feel I can no longer compete, I'll bow out,"* he says. The very word, compete, is a motif in his conversations with the press. While he loves the game, it's the head-to-head competition, the opportunity to differentiate himself from his peers, that gives him his edge. And there is also that upstart Tiger Woods to consider—a young man whose goal has been to eclipse the record set by Nicklaus. Jack has the utmost admiration for Tiger, and he probably knows that this young man will be the one to set new "unbreakable" records. However, one more major victory, especially if one of the casualties happened to be Eldrick Tiger Woods, would make the peak more difficult to scale.

"With the exception of one three-year period [1967-70], I feel I have become a better golfer every year since I took up the game at ten years of age. The better I have become, the more I have embarrassed myself by my failures, and the more I have embarrassed myself, the more I have been goaded into trying to develop greater skills. Of this I am presently certain: When failure ceases to embarrass me, and thus to stimulate me to greater efforts, my days will be done and I shall quit playing golf in public."

Jack Nicklaus

Can the Golden Bear still slug it out with the twentysomethings who drink mineral water and eat fruit and granola bars? Can an old forager with a fondness for sloppy burgers and Cokes still compete with the young Turks who pump iron and study yoga and have gurus to rearrange their auras? There's a voice inside Jack Nicklaus's skull that says, Yes. His way is the old way, the pure way...and he has a nearly Calvinistic belief that golf, while complex, relies on some very basic factors: a repeatable swing, a well-calculated plan, an understanding of course and conditions, and total concentration. While Arnold Palmer could magically extricate himself from phalanxed trees and knee-high rough, Jack's goal was to avoid such hazards in the first place. That was the essence of his game. To borrow a phrase from the medical profession, his first goal was always to do no harm.

In his heyday, Jack was among longest drivers on the tour, and one of the most accurate. His swing was compact and undramatic but powerful; his shot was a left-to-right fade, high and predictable. "The simpler the better," he's said time and time again. The essence of that "simple swing" philosophy is still evident in the way Nicklaus moves a clubhead through space—and time. He can, on occasion, still power a tee ball three hundred yards down the fairway, but his drives don't boom the way they used to.

"Sometimes the biggest problem is in your head. You've got to believe you can play a shot instead of wondering where your next bad shot is coming from."

Jack Nicklaus

When Jack overtook Palmer at the 1962 U.S. Open at Oakmont in Palmer's own backyard, ignoring the taunts of Arnie's Army, not to mention the untimely cheers accompanying his every misstep, the game had a new ruler, but an unwelcome one. Of course, Arnie was by no means finished, but the battle was duly joined and Arnie was now the underdog. Their rivalry was magnificent, and it endured for nearly a decade.

In his prime, Jack was as dominant as any golfer who ever lived, and within the city limits of Columbus, Ohio, heroically popular. Peter Jacobsen was paired with Jack at the former's own Memorial Tournament, held in the Golden Bear's hometown. On the last day, even fans who thought Jack was superhuman doubted he could snag the title—until the prestidigitator started to perform his magic. Shot after shot landed tight to the pin, resulting in a string of birdies that brought him from nowhere to the top of the leader board. Late in the round, when both Peter and Jack were lining up their putts,

Jack suggested politely that Peter go ahead and putt out of order. *"Why?"* Peter asked, eyeing Nicklaus's tricky fifteen-footer. *"Well,"* Jack said, *"When I make this, the crowd's going to go crazy."* The key word was *when*...not *if*. Shortly thereafter, the Bear promptly rolled in his long sidewinder, sending the crowd into a frenzy. Jack won the tournament, and in the process demonstrated the supreme confidence that made him unique.

Jack Nicklaus, even at age 19, was probably the best golfer in the world. Nobody really wanted to admit that truth, so popular was Arnold Palmer. When Palmer won the Masters in 1960, it was a chubby amateur from Ohio named Jack Nicklaus who was biting at his heels. When Palmer won the Cherry Hills U.S. Open that same year by shooting a final-round 65, it was Nicklaus who finished second. There was an inexorability to Jack's pursuit of Arnie's throne, but to those who loved Palmer, it seemed like a tragic coup d'etat.

Palmer, who occupied the throne from the late '50s until the early '60s, was a slasher whose preferred shot was a ripping draw that rolled forever down the fairway. The heir apparent, Jack Nicklaus, rather than adjust his stance to effect a draw or to exaggerate his fade, merely opened or closed the clubface slightly to create the proper bend. It was all so simple. And it worked. No histrionics there. Just pure logic. Their approach to the game was a manifestation of their personalities. For years these two very different athletes battled side by side, but now, as the horizon of youth narrows year by year and decade by decade, the two most significant players of the modern age are brought even closer by their shared mortality. When one or the other passes into the next realm, few will grieve more than Arnie for Jack or Jack for Arnie.

His formerly astonishing putting skills are now erratic. And the short game, never his forte, is further

diminished by the erosion of his fine motor skills. It happens, even to the best of us. But Jack Nicklaus

is such a superior golfer that, even compromised by the passage of time, he can summon up the old

magic on special occasions. And when he does, it is a marvel to behold. In 1998, at age 58, he was on

the leader board at the Masters until the final holes. He finished tenth, ahead of 135 golfers younger

than he, including Tiger Woods, the new king of golf.

"Success depends almost entirely on how effectively

you learn to manage the game's two ultimate

adversaries. The course and yourself."

Jack Nicklaus

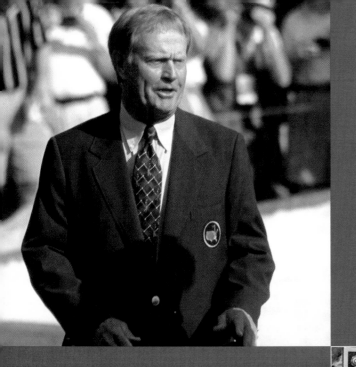

JACK NICKLAUS

IN 1963, JACK NICKLAUS, 23, WON HIS FIRST MASTERS TITLE AND BECAME THE TOURNAMENT'S YOUNGEST CHAMPION AT THAT TIME.

IN 1965, NICKLAUS SET TOURNAMENT RECORDS FOR SCORING (271) AND MARGIN OF VICTORY (NINE STROKES), INCLUDING A RECORD-TYING 64 IN THE THIRD ROUND. OF THIS PERFORMANCE, BOB JONES SAID, "JACK IS PLAYING AN ENTIRELY DIFFERENT GAME—A GAME WITH WHICH I'M NOT FAMILIAR."

NICKLAUS WON A THREE-WAY PLAYOFF IN 1966 AND BECAME THE FIRST CHAMPION TO SUCCESSFULLY DEFEND HIS MASTERS TITLE.

WITH HIS VICTORY IN 1972, NICKLAUS BECAME THE SECOND FOUR-TIME MASTERS CHAMPION.

DURING SUNDAY'S DRAMATIC FINAL ROUND IN 1975, NICKLAUS SANK A 40-FOOT BIRDIE PUTT AT NO. 16 THAT SECURED A ONE-STROKE VICTORY, EARNING HIM AN UNPRECEDENTED FIFTH GREEN JACKET.

IN 1986, AT AGE 46, NICKLAUS SCORED A FINAL ROUND 65, WHICH INCLUDED EAGLE-BIRDIE-BIRDIE AT HOLES 15, 16 AND 17, AND WON HIS SIXTH MASTERS. AT THAT TIME HE WAS THE OLDEST CHAMPION.

JACK NICKLAUS ELEVATED HIS GAME TO MEET GOLF'S CHALLENGES, INCLUDING THOSE AT THE MASTERS TOURNAMENT. THE MAN AND AUGUSTA NATIONAL GOLF CLUB WILL BE FOREVER LINKED.

DEDICATED APRIL 7, 1998

On the day before the opening round of the 1998 Masters, a tournament conceived by Bobby Jones to honor those who do credit to "the greatest game," the elder statesmen of golf paid tribute to Jack William Nicklaus in a moving, elegant ceremony. Jack Nicklaus, who had won the loyalty and admiration of golfing fans worldwide by virtue of nearly five decades of impeccable sportsmanship and brilliant play, accepted the award humbly, flanked by the legends of the game. The consummate traditionalist, he had finally received an accolade equivalent to knighthood in the realm of golf. Augusta was a fitting venue for the ceremony. Nicklaus, by his own account, had always played the game "as Bobby Jones would have wanted it to be played," with courage and skill. Nicklaus, eyes filled with tears, thanked his wife, his family, his friend and rival Arnold Palmer, and the heroic figures who had paved the way for him as the greatest golfer to date.

"*When you go head to head against Nicklaus, he knows he's going to beat you, you know he's going to beat you, and he knows you know he's going to beat you.*"

J.C. Snead

"I knew exactly how intimidating I was to most of the other players. And it gave me a huge competitive edge. I knew that if I kept the pressure on and didn't do anything stupid, I would often win.

"This might sound like arrogance, but it really wasn't. I recognized that many of my opponents had physical skills equal or even superior to mine, but I also knew that few of them had the mental or emotional capability to use them as effectively as I generally could mine. Somebody might up and simply beat me, as Lee Trevino and Tom Watson did a number of times, but I was totally confident that I would not beat myself once I had gotten into a winning position.

"The truth is that most players give tournaments away, particularly major championships. In at least a third of my Majors wins, I was simply there to accept the gift."

Jack Nicklaus

"In retrospect, if I had to do it all over again, I would still go as hard as I could after the same result, but with more effort to disguise the intensity or rawness of my will to win. At the age of twenty-two, it simply never occurred to me how apparent this was in the way I went about the game, nor that some people might interpret it as coldness of heart or bleakness of spirit. In short, although the goals I set myself probably were acceptable to everyone—maybe even to many of Arnie's Army—the fact is I marched toward them along too straight and narrow a path for the majority of observers to want to applaud my passage. My focus was too sharp, too internalized, too locked on where I wanted to go, to recognize and cater to the fact that I was in the entertainment business as much as the golf-playing business. And it was this, I'm sure, that made me such a black hat to so many of the fans for so many of those early years. Sure, I was overweight and crew-cut, and sure, I dressed like a guy painting a porch, and sure, I had a squeaky voice and didn't laugh and joke a lot in public, and sure, I often lacked tact and diplomacy in my public utterances. I believe all of those failings might have been forgiven a young and unsophisticated individual if he had simply papered over the raw intensity of his will to win."

Jack Nicklaus

How peculiar it must be for Jack Nicklaus to have dominated the golfing scene for thirty years, winning major tournaments in four decades, and now admit that the magical skills are on the wane. He glances at the calendar from time to time but seems only to notice that there are still pages left to be turned. While it might be too much to hope that Arnie could have that one miraculous weekend that could erase the realities of age and mortality, Jack's enduring skills are such that he might just thrill us once again. That is every golfing fan's hope whenever the Bear strides onto the first tee at Augusta or Shinnecock or St. Andrews. Jack has something to prove; a fire still burns in his ample belly. Next year, 2000, he will be back in the hunt at the Masters, and presumably the U.S. Open, the British Open and the PGA. With his new titanium hip and his new titanium driver, maybe, just maybe, the Golden Bear will roar again. One can only hope.

Tom Watson

This year's British Open was held at Carnoustie, hard by the Kingdom of Fife and a mere caber toss from the birthplace of golf, St. Andrews. Once again, Tom Watson flew across the Atlantic, this time to compete for his sixth British Open Championship, although neither his game nor his ailing shoulder was totally up to the task. Thus, *Carnasty*, as it was dubbed, got the better of him. In typical Watson fashion, no mention was made of the injury prior to the event; excuses have never been part of Watson's mindset. Injuries are components of the game...like deep roughs or immovable impediments. One simply makes the best of things and moves on. During the week prior to the tournament he stopped in Ireland to play some of the great seaside courses near and dear to his heart. I happened to be playing Ballybunion on the day Watson arrived to have a go at this wonderful links, which threads through massive, shaggy dunes. There was a buzz amongst the caddies and clubhouse personnel, as if the Pope himself were arriving to bless the masses. I was well into my own bogey-laden round when Watson teed off, although I occasionally caught a glimpse of him and the several hundred fans who trailed along with his group. I asked Danny, my wee, wizened caddie, if he'd ever carried Watson's bag. *"No,"* he said. *"The professional bag is big as a corpse. But for him I'd gladly straggle 'round with it. It would be a great honor. He's a fine man, Tom Watson."* The Celts, who know and love golf, have the utmost respect for this thirty-year tour veteran because he honors traditions that still thrive on the ancient, hallowed courses in the Gaelic regions. He is a purist, a true student of the game, who would likely be a happy man in any walk of life so long as he could play golf, which he loves so much.

"No other game combines the wonder of nature with the discipline of sport in such a carefully planned way. A great golf course both frees and challenges a golfer's mind."

Tom Watson

"The fewer moving parts there are, the simpler and more consistent your method will probably be."

David Leadbetter

Unfortunately, Pros nowadays have access to amenities and rewards unheard of in the era of Snead and Hogan and Nelson, when even access to the clubhouse was a rarity. They have sports psychologists, personal coaches, physical therapists, technicians, first-class clubhouse facilites, fabulous purses, perfect venues, and unlimited choices of clubs, balls, shoes and garb. They sometimes lose sight of their obligations in favor of mercenary

concerns. Not so with Watson, who is seldom too busy to sign autographs or to help an

amateur playing partner line up a putt. He is courteous to the press, even under trying

circumstances when most pros would be hiding in a bunker. And like Bobby Jones before

him, Tom Watson is highly literate and intellectually acute. Only Jack Nicklaus is in his class

when it comes to analyzing the character of a golf course, then adapting his own proclivities

to the task at hand.

"It's funny how little things stick in a man's mind. One of my first memories of Tom Watson is from the 1974 Jackie Gleason Inverrary Classic, and it had nothing to do with the tournament. On Wednesday, the day of the pro-am, I was driving my car to the club when I happened to glance over at a course near Inverrary Country Club. All alone in a practice bunker was Tom Watson, a green kid who, I'd been told, hit the ball too wildly to last on the PGA Tour. I barely noticed. I went ahead and played my round in the pro-am. But when I left the course five hours later, I looked over at that golf course and damn if Watson wasn't in the same bunker, still practicing sand shots."

Lee Trevino

Despite the fact that Thomas Sturges Watson is a quiet workhorse, a "grinder," on the tour, he has been a protagonist in some of the most indelible and important scenes in the history of golf.

Consider his miraculous chip-in birdie to win the 1982 U.S. Open at Pebble Beach, nudging Jack Nicklaus by a single stroke. Who can forget the image of Tom Watson dashing ecstatically down the slope onto the green, putter aloft, pointing affirmatively at his caddie: *"Told you,"* he is saying. Nicklaus waited patiently for his rival to hit his chip shot at Pebble Beach's 18th hole, and when the deed was done he put his arm around Tom's shoulder and said, *"You did it again, you little S.O.B."* As the old adage goes, the truest words are spoken in jest. Watson had done it, just as he had done it at Turnberry in 1977. There's no doubt that Jack would sooner have lost to Watson than to any other golfer, such was his admiration for the man. It is Watson's only U.S. Open victory to date, but one of the finest finishes in the history of the sport. And back in that 1977 Open at Turnberry, he and Jack, having traded birdies back and forth throughout the incoming nine, staggered up the fairway of the 72nd hole, arms around each other like two weary heavyweights at the end of a hard-fought championship bout. Watson won that particular battle, but the contest was so magnificent that neither of the two could possibly be considered a loser. Watson was the victor, to be sure, but no one lost. Tom has said many times that the '77 British Open was a watershed experience, after which he knew he could compete with the best player in the world. That event undoubtedly certified in Jack Nicklaus's mind that a noble and worthy adversary had arrived on the scene. They relish the head-to-head battle about as much as they treasure victory. It's a hard concept for most of their contemporaries to fully appreciate, but rarely do such rivalries exist nowadays when there are dozens of golfers at the top echelon of the sport.

95

Millions of practice balls have grooved his swing into a highly repeatable stroke, every bit as effective now as then. Even as he approaches his fiftieth birthday, Watson is arguably the most consistent ball striker on the tour. If the rest of his game is "on"—that is, if the flat stick is cooperating—he will be a strong contender! It is as simple as that. In his prime, Watson was a wonderfully bold putter; however, for the past decade the putt has been the bane of his existence. Maybe it's the traditionalist in him that prevents his resorting to the long putter so popular on the senior tour.

"I lived by the putter earlier in my career. I died by it today."

(After losing the 1994 AT&T Pro-Am at Pebble Beach to

Johnny Miller.)

Tom Watson

"I always had a lot of confidence in my putting. I could make it from everywhere.

"I miss a lot of short putts now compared with then, when I missed very few. I used to make 20-, 30-, 40-, 50-footers. I remember playing in the Hawaiian Open with Doug Sander. I made two 30-footers and a 40-footer on the last three holes. That didn't surprise me too much. I mean, I had the line, I hit the ball where I was looking, and the ball went in the hole. But that doesn't occur now. I have a hard time seeing the line now. I started losing it when I was about 22, 23. Up until that time, I was amazing. I aimed the putter and I knew the ball was going right along that line. By instinct you know it is the line of the putt. You know how much it breaks; you know exactly how to hit it. The way I putt, I determine how much it's going to break, and then I pick a point to the right or left of the hole and aim at that point. I play a straight putt at that point. I just can't see that line nearly as well anymore."

Tom Watson

These days, Watson is not a flashy figure on the fairways. But in the '70s and '80s he fell prey to the lurid fashions of the day. He donned cringeworthy plaid bell-bottoms and garish shirts of painful hues, but such finery seemed to contradict his workmanlike approach to golf. His scraggly hair was blatantly au courant, true, yet beneath the unfortunate raiments was a deliberate technician whose compact motion was a powerful first cousin to that of Gene "The Machine" Littler, one of his boyhood idols.

"The man [Watson] simply burned to win and, within the rules, was prepared to pay whatever price was necessary to do so, and that quality just oozed from his body language whenver he was at full bore."

Jack Nicklaus

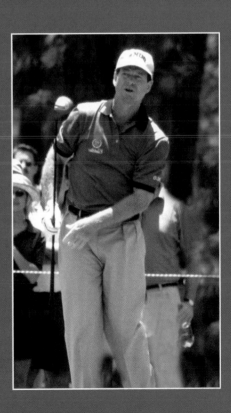

Tom Watson is a throwback to the graceful days when golf was strictly the domain of gentlemen and ladies, when decorum, integrity and sportsmanship were the hallmarks. He is the inheritor of Bobby Jones's code, in which reverence for the game is the guiding principle: fans, weekend golfers, officials, volunteers, and fellow competitors deserve and receive honor and consideration; they are regarded as integral constituents in the very fabric of the sport. Jones never turned professional, and he appreciated the fact that without fans and weekend golfers, the context for golf at the professional level would evaporate. Thus, he made himself available to a public who adored him. As a player, Jones, like Watson, rarely complained about course conditions when he competed, believing there was nothing to be gained from doing so when every competing golfer played the same eighteen holes as he. Furthermore, Jones felt that any such grousing might cost some poor groundskeeper his job at a time when jobs were hard to come by. In order to broaden the game's appeal, he made some of the best instructional films ever produced, wrote lovingly about the game so near to his heart, extolled the virtues of golf course architecture as an art form, and created the Masters Tournament at Augusta National where ritual and ceremony are seemingly changeless. Bobby Jones lived to see Watson at his best and heartily approved of the character and quality of his approach to the game of golf. When Tom won his first Masters in 1977, Bobby Jones was there at the end to shake his hand.

"When Tom was winning everything, I heard him say something at a clinic that went to the heart of his positive attitude. He said it never bothered him to miss a green because one of four things could happen, and three of them were good: he could hole the shot from off the green or out of the bunker, he could hit it close and tap in, he could hit it poorly and make a good putt, or he could hit it poorly and miss the putt. He said if you added up all those scores—a birdie, two pars, and a bogey—it came to even-par. So if you practiced your short game, you had nothing to fear."

Peter Jacobsen

"When I was at the top of my game, I got my comeuppance about autographs. I was walking out of the locker room at Firestone with a hanging bag over my shoulder. I was rushing to a plane, and this little kid comes up to me and asks me for my autograph. I said, "No, son, can't you see my hands are full?" And his father was there and he called me an ——hole. I went face-to-face with him and said, "What did you call me?" He said, "You are an ——hole." I couldn't say anything to him. I just walked away.

But he was right. There was a little kid who wanted my autograph, who looked up at me with those eyes, and when I turned him down he looked at me with astonishment. I hurt him."

Tom Watson

At age 48, Tom Watson won the 1998 Honda Colonial Classic in Fort Worth, Texas. He was the oldest player ever to have won that tournament. It was the cap on a splendid year that brought him back to the forefront of the American golfing scene. Thanks to a new physical fitness regimen and the loss of fifteen pounds, Huck Finn is back in fighting trim and ready to compete at the highest levels. There will be many other tournaments and majors down the road, and, of course, the young guns will be highly favored to take home the trophy. But one would be unwise to bet the deed to the farm against Watson's chances. If sheer dogged determination can win a tournament, Watson has a surprise or two for those doubters among us. We are all the luckier for his reemergence.

"We learn our life from others. I have learned from my father how to hit a golf shot, how to act on a golf course, what the etiquette is. I learned from David Leadbetter how to keep my left arm closer to my side. I have learned from Jack Nicklaus by watching him hit a six-iron to the seventeenth hole at Hawaii rather than a five-iron. Why? Because he wanted to take all risk out of it. I learned from Arnold Palmer how to treat people."

Tom Watson

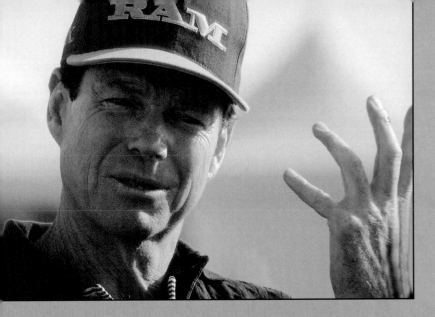

In addition to winning eight Majors, Watson was a regular participant in the biannual Ryder Cup competition. He was entrusted with the captaincy of the 1993 team, which defeated the Europeans in a highly emotional, hard-fought contest whose outcome was determined by Bernhard Langer's missed final putt on the last hole. It was a comeback win for the American team, and the product of shrewd pairings on the part of Captain Watson.

Watson has eschewed the technicolor clothing of the 70s in favor of conservative slacks and understated shirts. His hair is short and time has worn channels in his freckled skin, but the gap-toothed smile is as broad and sincere as ever, and the look of determination still flames in his eyes. There is no player on the tour more respected or universally liked than Watson. His character is as rock-solid as his swing. There is little of the gamesmanship so evident when Nicklaus and Palmer were locked in combat. Instead, there is a quiet, head-down determination built into his approach to the game. His philosophy seems to be summed up by Polonius' words to his son Laertes in Shakespeare's *Hamlet*: *"This above all, to thine own self be true."*

Greg Norman

Consider the life of a shark. Not just any shark, but the Shark, as in Greg Norman. Of all the players on the tour, Norman is the one you could imagine drinking beer with at the local pub. You'd laugh a lot, whack each other on the back, clink your pint glasses together, laugh some more. "You said it, mate." He'd be one bloke you'd want on your side should some drunk find the cut of your jib sufficiently objectionable as to provoke fisticuffs. "Get 'im, Greg," you'd say, and run for the phone to dial 911. It would not be pretty.

Like many of the other affable Aussies playing the American tour, Norman lives in Florida, not far from Orlando, which is home to his good friend and idol, Jack Nicklaus, not to mention Mark O'Meara and Tiger Woods. Early in his career, he was known to have a pint or two at the end of a hard day's grind on the golf course. It was the Aussie way. Now, as a family man, he cuts loose by flying his own plane or driving one of his several Ferraris up and down the back roads of his adopted state. But he's an Aussie at heart, and he returns home often to play in tournaments in his native country, where he is regarded as a hero. When the tournament is over, he hunts wild game in the Outback with friends.

"There are several good ways to swing at a golf ball,

but only one good way to play golf—aggressively."

Greg Norman

When Greg Norman was a kid growing up in Brisbane, Australia, golf was the furthest thing from his mind. He was a surfer god, blond and muscular, a football hunk ready to mix it up with his mates. A risk taker. Golf, to his way of thinking, was for ladies, evidenced by his mother's passion for the game. He wasn't averse to toting her clubs from time to time, and the strategies they discussed were vaguely appealing, but for a young tough who loved the hurly-burly sports played in a vat of testosterone, golf seemed effeminate, and altogether too genteel. That is, until Jack Nicklaus began making headlines worldwide. Norman identified with the Golden Bear's powerful approach to the game of golf. His mother, perhaps seizing the moment, bought him Nicklaus's book, *Golf My Way*, and the rest, as they say, is history. Greg channeled his hormones and his athleticism into the sport he had rejected out of hand. He abandoned his surfboard and his Aussie football cleats in favor of golf clubs; then, dutifully subscribing to the techniques set forth in Nicklaus's book, worked his handicap down from the twenties to scratch in one year. In a breathtakingly short span of time he had achieved his first significant success on the Australian Tour. After joining the PGA Tour in 1983, Norman hired Butch Harmon, currently Tiger Woods's mentor, but he's now coached by David Leadbetter, considered by many the top guru in golf. Local newspapers nicknamed Norman Little Bear. However, Greg recognized the fact that one bear was enough, and rejected the moniker.

"The mind follows

the body."

Greg Norman

Norman is a jock par excellence and a formidable presence on and off the golf course. There's that remarkable silhouette, featuring shoulders wider than most doorways and the slender hips of a college halfback. In an age when the overweight Billy Mayfair and Tim Herrin, or tiny technicians like Pavin and Leonard and Kite are often the physical prototype, Norman cuts a scary figure indeed, swaggering purposefully down the center of the fairway, all six feet plus of him. Yet despite his intimidating appearance, Greg Norman is one of the nicest guys on the tour, and surely one of the best sportsmen playing the game today.

The camera loves Greg Norman the way it loved Palmer. He has become identified with a broad-brimmed black mesh hat and shirts with strident graphics set against solid backgrounds. Then there's the silver-tipped leather belt, a Norman trademark. Among so many stoics, guys like Leonard, Duval and Mickelson, the volcanic temperament of the Shark makes for good theater. Thanks to some clever marketing strategies by the International Management Group, the Shark logo appears on a line of clothing and golfing paraphernalia. An investment of $1.9 million ten years ago in Cobra has recently returned $42 million to the Great White Shark. If on occasion he falters on the course, he never does so in his commercial ventures. Aside from being the all-time top earning professional golfer on the PGA Tour ($12 million), Greg Norman has masterminded a vastly remunerative commercial enterprise, for which he is the walking advertisement.

"Before I'm thirty, I'll be a millionaire, I'll be the best golfer in the world and I'll be married to an American."

Greg Norman

(10 years later he would accomplish all of the above

It's only fitting that late in 1983 Jack Nicklaus himself talked Norman into joining the PGA tour, although the Shark's first victory came a full two years later. Thereafter he was a consistent winner on the PGA tour, racking up 18 victories in North America and 56 more overseas. He became known as the Shark early on, thanks to a newspaper reporter who amalgamated the various predatory attributes of the young Aussie into an emblem that fit him perfectly. More than any other golfer, he lurks just beneath the surface, somewhere near the lead, capable at any point in the final round of savaging his opponents and shredding the golf course in the process. Greg Norman seized upon the fortuitous nickname at a time when the movie *Jaws* spawned worldwide shark mania.

Nick Price, perhaps his closest friend on the U.S. Tour, believes Norman's place in the golfing pantheon is right below Jack Nicklaus. Greg, he says, is great because he manages, despite his magnificent failures, to come back time and time again, always positioning himself for dramatic victory and glorious defeat. And Greg Norman himself suggests that what makes golf thrilling is not so much the wins as the losses, which put a man's humanity and grace on public display.

Of course, given the Oedipal curse hovering over him, he has had more practice than most at being a gracious loser. His run of bad luck and self-immolations has been well documented, but here's a brief sampler. He's had eight second-place finishes in the majors (compared to just two victories, both British Open crowns); he lost the '84 U.S. Open by cratering in a playoff with Fuzzy Zoeller; in 1986 he forfeited the Masters to Jack Nicklaus by pushing a 4-iron approach into the bleachers at the final hole; that same year, Bob Tway canned a bunker shot on the 18th hole to edge Norman in the PGA; in 1987, Larry Mize snatched the Masters from Norman by chipping in from 100 feet. The saga is almost too painful, although there are many more chapters in this tale of woe. He has thrown away huge leads time and time again, lost play-offs and generally improvised various means of avoiding victory. But always, *always,* he has maintained his good cheer and philosophical moorings.

"The failure is what makes succeeding so sweet," he says. "In golf, failure is a great thing— an absolutely necesssary thing. The idea of failure is, I think, my driving force."

On the other hand, he obliterated the field in the 1986 British Open at Turnberry and again in 1993 at Royal St. George's. The obvious conclusion to be drawn from Norman's almost schizophrenic performance in major tournaments is that his swing is perhaps too tied to his emotions. This might, in some quarters, be construed as a knock on his golf game; but his human frailty makes him seem more like the rest of us, and we love him all the more for his vulnerability.

"When you don't stand up to pressure, that's golf, that's life. One of my dearest friends is Nigel Mansell, the racing driver, and he and I can relate to that a little bit because it's happened to him in the Grand Prix world, and it's happened to me in the golf world. You feel like you have the thing in your grasp, right at the end of your fingertips, then you can't grasp all of it, and it's gone.... You can't control what other people do...you can only control your own destiny.... In the end you both see the light, and decide, well this is the sport I am in, and that's the name of the game."

Greg Norman

During the 1992 Tour, Norman's outlook and psyche changed dramatically when he incorporated a serious diet into

his routine along with a physical fitness program. He often spends up to two hours a day in the gym. He was pleased with

his "Fit for Life" diet when he lost fifteen pounds by giving up soft drinks and other goodies. When Norman decimated

his field of competitors in the 1993 Doral and won by four strokes, Gary Van Sickle of *Golf World* wrote, *"Mark it down,*

folks: the sulking, frowning, irritable, sensitive Norman of the past two years is history! The often spectacular, fun-loving,

outgoing, happy-go-lucky warrior, the Great White Shark, who was a dominant force in the late '80s is back."

Greg Norman is in all things a contradiction: jovial but ruthless, hugely talented but vulnerable to his own emotions, laid-back but highly temperamental. Back in Norman's globe-trotting heyday, on a rainy afternoon in Hong Kong after a two-day postponement due to rain, his road manager entered the Shark's hotel room and discovered him hitting leisurely golf balls through an open window into Hong Kong's magnificent harbor. Perhaps his target was the red sail of a junk inching its way across the seascape, or the mast of a luxurious sailing ship. It's easy to imagine Greg and his manager sharing a hearty laugh, not to mention a casual beer. "Practice is practice, mate," he might have said. Then when the rains gave way to sunshine and the tournament reached its conclusion a few days later, the Shark just as casually devoured his opponents.

His demeanor changes when the competitive juices are flowing. He purses his lips, glares at the flag, flashes his gleaming teeth, clenches his jaw in fierce concentration. In short, the Shark becomes a hunter. Fans gravitate towards a player whom they feel they know, and Norman is a kind of everyman who hides little from his fans—or at least that is the impression he creates. So, when he suffers his tragic downfalls, we identify with him as did the ancient Greeks with their cursed kings and doomed warriors. When he triumphs over his foes, we identify with his conquest.

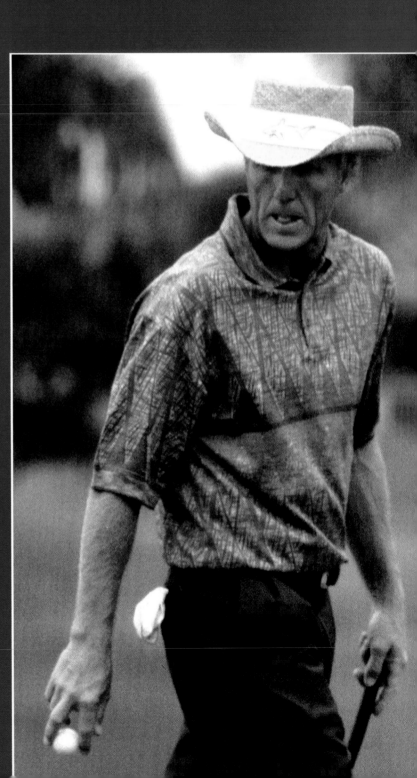

143

"When I play golf, I treat every single stroke—during a tournament as much as during a friendly game—as if my life depended on it. When I go hunting or fishing, I'd like to think that I am better at it than anybody else, because I approach everthing I do in life as uncompromisingly as I play golf."

Greg Norman

Norman's craggy, weather-beaten face, his surfer hair, his shiny artificial chompers, and his hawk's beak make him one of the most identifiable characters ever to play the game. His early involvement in dangerous sports has carried over to his golf game, where he has always been a risk-taker. Sometimes this proclivity blows up in his face, but mostly it works to his advantage. His swing is reckless-looking yet incredibly precise, evidenced by his consistently high standing in the PGA's driving-accuracy statistics.

His collection of Ferraris is a perfect metaphor for someone like Greg Norman, who is always on the go, from dawn to dusk. His calendar is filled with appearances, business obligations, charity events, golf tournaments, and consultations with his thriving golf course design group. Whether he is fleeing from a flash storm on the golf course or piloting his helicopter through the Everglades for his own amusement, toying with Indy cars at astronomical speeds or playing with sharks from inside a steel cage many fathoms deep, he is being Greg Norman, and doing it with style. He is a veritable blur, whether or not he's roaring across the landscape. As Steve Elkington, a countryman and buddy of Norman's, states, *"Greg likes to stand right on the edge of the cliff."*

Now, healing from shoulder surgery, the Shark has once again entered the competitive fray. He led the 1999 Masters through the third round, then faltered. He failed to make the cut at the U.S. Open, then wrought havoc again at the British Open, much to the delight of his loyal fans. Now, predictably, the Shark is swimming again, circling, threatening to surface and rock the boat. Sports writers and fellow golfers will once again foolishly consign Greg Norman to history and he will confound them. Those who choose to swim with sharks had best beware.

Tiger Woods

In the weird light trained upon him by journalists, soothsayers, corporate entities and fans alike, Eldrick Tiger Woods is growing up. Superficially, this new Tiger is a more muscular, more durable version of the willowy young man who assumed center stage a couple of years ago at Augusta. His biceps bulge beneath his shirtsleeves, and his chest seems thicker than before, making him an even more intimidating presence on the golf course.

But the real growth is evident in how this phenomenal young man has adapted to the rigors of fame, fortune, and universally high expectations—especially his own! And if his life is an open book, he at least has the option now of choosing the page to which the world will have access. You could begin to see the transformation sometime during the 1999 U.S. Open at Pinehurst #2 with its fiendishly undulating greens, where patience and acceptance were paramount. More than once, the rub of the green worked against him, and on those occasions Tiger merely shrugged off his misfortune and moved to the next hole. Perhaps his caddie, Steve Williams, a young man with cool optimism, has provided a kind of stabilizing influence that his former caddie, Fluff Cowen the loveable smurf, could not. Or maybe the maturation process can be attributed to the mere passage of time and accumulating layers of experience, both on and off the golf course.

Where before he was likely to force any issue he confronted, Tiger now seems happy to let things happen as they will. He has seemingly come to realize that, although he stands a better chance than any man alive of winning a given golf tournament, the likelihood is that he will not. In August 1999 at Medina Country Club, Tiger sank a clutch putt on the 17th hole to outlast the hard-charging adolescent from Spain, Sergio Garcia, to win the PGA. The drama of Sergio's superb play over the last several holes nearly overshadowed Tiger's steady, purposeful command of the task at hand. After having holed out on 18, Tiger seemed more exhausted than ecstatic. It was a hard-working, hard-fought victory of the sort that only a mature golfer could capture. Could it be that he has discovered the virtues of a philosophical mind-set, that secret ingredient of great achievement? Has he been lying awake at night poring over the writings of Bobby and Sam and Ben and Jack? Maybe so. Did Shivas Irons visit him in a dream? Undoubtedly.

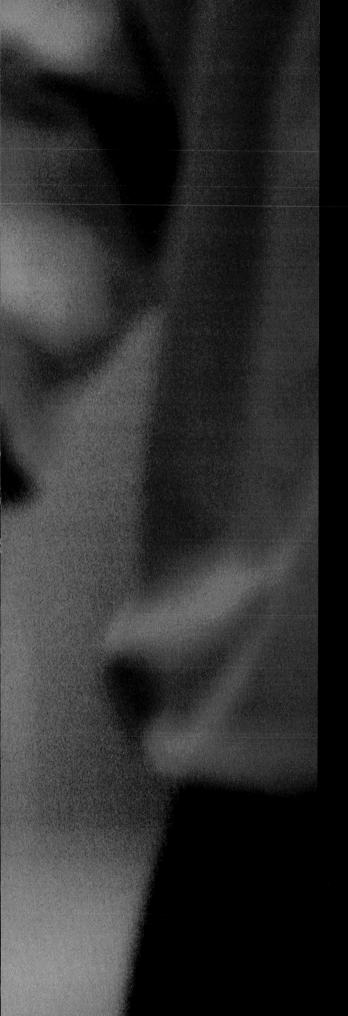

Eldrick Tiger Woods was never unknown to true golf aficionados, who first saw him at age three on The Mike Douglas Show clowning with Bob Hope on a makeshift AstroTurf putting green under the watchful gaze of his ubiquitous stage father Earl Woods. Even then, there was a quality to young Tiger's presence before the camera as he cheated his ball toward the well-choreographed forays into the public eye, in whose periphery he remained until he filled the landscape with his scintillating talents at the most significant amateur events, including an impossible three successive U.S. Junior Amateur Championships, followed by three consecutive U.S. Amateur Titles, the last of which was the historic comeback of comebacks at the 1996 event held at Pupmpkin Ridge.

It was Earl Woods, a Green Beret officer in the 1960s, who named his son Tiger after a cherished friend, Vietnamese Lieutenant Colonel Nguyen Phong, notorious in battle and legendary among his troops. Tiger Woods was born on December 30, 1975, in Cypress, California, to Earl and his Thai wife Kultida. One can only assume that the baby was immediately handed a driver and golf ball by his father, who early on saw that his son was something quite special—golf's chosen one, perhaps, with influence radiating beyond the game into the social and political realm. Some of Earl's pronouncements seem grandiose; then again, Tiger Woods has always defied belief. Will his accomplishments eclipse those of Jack Nicklaus, whose career Tiger closely monitored? As The Golden Bear himself has publicly stated, *"Arnold and I agree that you could take his Masters and my Masters and add them together, and this kid should win more than that!"* There will be many day-to-day rivals to challenge for any given tournament, but Tiger Woods's only real competitor is his own looming legend, Jack Nicklaus.

After winning the 1997 Masters Tournament by a record 12 shots over Tom Kite, his closest rival, Eldrick Tiger Woods, towel draped around his neck, told press-tent reporters that he did so without benefit of his "A" game. I, like a vast number of American males and a fair share of admiring women, was sitting in a living room at the time, sipping something frosty, watching Tiger behind the microphone. He was obviously reveling in the afterglow of his victory, perhaps no more in command of his utterances than he was after having shot an inexplicable front side 40 on day one of the tournament.

So what was he trying to prove with his immodest press conference statement? I wondered what the fallout would be among his peers, who had plenty of reasons to be jealous without this sort of incentive. The comment went down poorly indeed, especially considering that his fellow professionals had spent four days gazing into his afterburners as he sped away from them toward certain victory. Some of them found his words insulting, others deemed them arrogant; the most generous of his fellow pros found the comment to be thoughtless. And many of them said so publicly. The criticism stung Tiger Woods, and he took the matter to heart. He apologized for any offense he might have given, tried to put the statement in "context," and eventually distanced himself from the obvious implications of his words. It was a stark initiation into a fraternity with rigid protocols and a nearly ritualized decorum.

Still, you couldn't help wondering...was he that much better than the mere mortals who had toiled amongst the azaleas and dogwoods on the hallowed turf of Augusta National? Nowadays you have to concede that the answer is probably yes.

One interesting footnote to his exploits at Augusta in 1997 is worth repeating. Like many of his competitors, Tiger had rented a house near the golf course for the entire Masters week. And after the tournament was over, the Woods family threw a big party for friends and a few of his fellow golfers. Because Tiger was emotionally exhausted from his victory, the party wound down at a reasonable hour, earlier than one straggler had anticipated. He entered the house and, seeing only Tida, Earl and a few durable guests standing in the kitchen, began searching the various rooms for the young man who had conquered Augusta. He opened Tiger's bedroom door and found him sprawled on his king-size bed, fast asleep, clutching his green Masters Jacket.

Except for some bad luck on the greens at Pinehurst's exacting #2 Course, Tiger would have won the 1999 U.S. Open. And for weeks after the tournament he methodically dismantled the fields at several tournaments leading up to the British Open at Carnoustie. In the years following his brash post-Masters comments, Eldrick Tiger Woods has come of age as a player and as a person. Despite the wilting glare of public scrutiny, Tiger has finally accepted the idea that the people genuinely like him, that they admire his abilities, that he has nothing to prove except to himself. Even Earl has moved from center stage to the background, which is all to the good.

We see Tiger nattily dressed like a young exec in his role as a multimillion-dollar spokesman for American Express. He stars in Nike commercials where we see a different persona, the charismatic superstar. This particular sponsor remunerates its standard bearer to the tune of $40 million. We want to know him, but his larger-than-life public image prohibits any sort of intimacy, real or imagined; his pre-packaged brand of charisma may thrill us, but it doesn't invite us in.

The marketing strategies are often aimed at Wheaties-gobbling children, who idolize Tiger Woods, decorate their rooms with stuffed Bengals and crowd the ropes at tournament venues, hoping for an autograph or a pat on the head from Tiger. While he purports to be a role model for the youth of the nation, he has become less accessible to his adoring fans over the past couple of years, possibly for the sake of self-preservation. We now see the Tiger he wants us to see, on his terms, on a

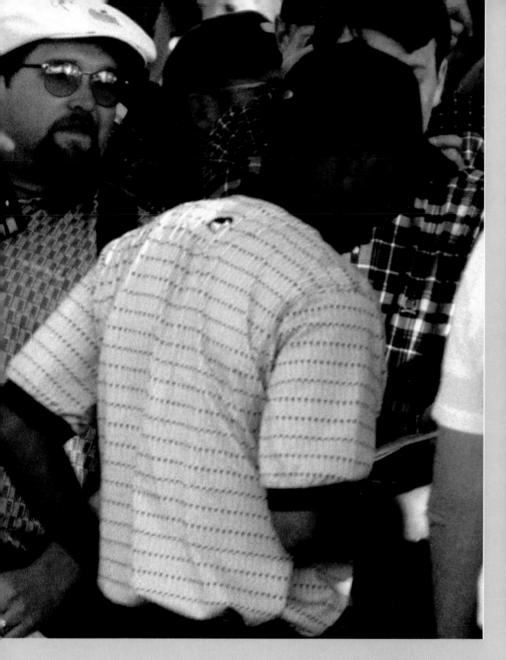 

carefully crafted stage. Which is not to say that he has turned his back on his public responsibilities. He underwrites the Tiger Woods Foundation, whose goal is to provide inner-city kids with training and golf equipment, not to mention access to golf courses. Kids adore him, in part because his name is Tiger, rather than Eugene or Milton. The bottom-line explaination has to do with that all too rare commodity: charisma.

Off the golf course Tiger Woods looks like a college kid on spring break. Blue jeans and tee-shirts, hat backwards, an easy laugh, a big smile. Woods goes to movies, drinks beer and probably thinks about things besides golf. But with a very few exceptions, notably his caddie Steve Williams, his former Stanford teammate Gerry Chang, his coach Butch Harmon and his Dad, nobody really knows Tiger, or even thinks they know him the way they do Palmer or Norman. In Tiger's case we're presented with a persona—that of an arch-competitor who can toss clubs in anger, berate impolite fans or photographers (or himself) with a few choice words, laugh at his blunders, charge himself up when the pressure is on, close himself off from the word around him when there's a putt to be made or a crucial recovery shot to be executed....

"I've never tried to emulate one person. Every person has faults. I've tried to adopt the best attributes of many people. I've always studied great players. They were great for a reason. I like to find out why they were great. I used to love to watch Tom Watson putt, Trevino hit little wedges, or Nicklaus hit long irons. I would watch how they did it and why. More important, I like to study their decision-making on the golf course. I've tried to pick fifty players and combine the best of them, and to make one super player."

Tiger Woods

"You da man," they shout. *"You da man, Tiger."* The phrase rolls across the green terrain.

Years ago, other men cast their legendary shadows on much humbler fairways, men unknown

to most of us who love the game: Rhodes, Elder, Sifford, and Thorpe. Pioneers who persevered

and paved the way. Now the man who strides the emerald fairways, illuminated by a brilliant sun,

is master of a sport so long denied to men like him until its own emancipation.

"God gave me a gift. And he trusted me to take care of it."

Earl Woods

"Pop wears many hats in our relationship. He is my counselor, my coach, my conscience, my inspiration, and my hero. He is an invaluable, indespensable and irreplaceable player on 'Team Tiger.' Without his friendship, guidance, and support, I would not be where I am today."

Tiger Woods

His son becomes the man he might have been, had the world been different way back when. How wistful to imagine his younger self walking these fairways, arcing nine irons stiff to the pin, tapping in for birdie. The crowd cheers; and Tiger waves for both of them.

Each and every emotion is evident on his face. David Duval, Davis Love, Freddy Couples, Justin Leonard, Phil Mickelson—most of Tiger's major rivals, in fact—are taciturn at best, dull at worst.

This year's incarnation is more confident and more affable. He is by nature a demonstrative player; he pumps his fist, screams, feeds off of the crowds who adore him.

On the tees, on the fairways, or on the greens, wherever he can steal a few quiet moments, he seems to enter a tunnel of concentration inaccessible to mere mortals

"Tiger Woods is the most important golfer to come along in fifty years.

Tom Watson

Tiger has joined Seve Ballesteros as one of the most imaginative and effective short-game players of all time. He chips with his three wood, swings his lob wedge full bore from greenside rough,

slashes low draws beneath tree limbs, owns the sand as surely as any Bedouin tribesman, and generally finds the means to get the ball on the green from almost any place on the golf course.

Anyone who has seen Tiger Woods in the flesh can verify that there is a sort of magic that envelops him. He has the delicate hands of an artist, and the graceful gait of a dancer.

His 90 compression Titleist soars impossible distances and lands softly mid-fairway often enough to give him an enormous edge on his opponents. He hits eight irons farther than some of his fellow pros hit their five irons. And when he finds that mystical zone, when his reads are precise, his putting can be supernatural.

After the round is over, Butch reviews the pluses and minuses with his student. How strange to imagine that anyone can have the wisdom (or temerity) to make changes to the most effective swing in golf. Who looked over Van Gogh's shoulder when his lavish strokes went awry, and who scolded Arthur Rubenstein if his technique faltered? It was their passion that guided their instincts. And such is the case with a golfing genius like Eldrick Tiger Woods.

Butch Harmon, the key figure in the entourage, usually coptors in with his protégé for practice rounds. He studies Tiger's majestic swing, tweaks it here, adjusts the wrist cock, the takeaway, fine-tunes the angle of attack. Sometimes he can be seen standing in the fog, near the practice bunker, or behind a pyramid of practice balls, stroking his chin, scrutinizing the variables of a swing unlike any other in golf.

When you come right down to it, a professional golfer is a species of bigamist. He is married to at least three, and possibly four, different spouses at once. First the game itself, but also to his caddie and his coach. (He might also have a wife with whom to share his triumphs and losses, although, as yet. Tiger seems not to have found his romantic soul-mate.) The Woods/Harmon relationship is based on loyalty, faith, love and trust, the essence of any great marriage. Occasionally there is a divorce or two along the way. Fluff, the frumpy Sancho Panza, was let go during the 1998-1999 off-season in favor of a less conspicuous personality, Steve Williams.

Now, in 1999, having won the PGA, his star is once again at the center of the golfing firmament. He

enters this year's Ryder Cup at the top of his game. A head-to-head match with the talented teen, Sergio

Garcia, is inevitable. Such a contest may bring televised golf to a new level of popularity, and might just

elevate the Ryder Cup to the status of the Super Bowl or the Final Four.

The 1999 British Open is history. A Scotsman who grew up just down the road from Carnoustie won the Claret Jug this year, but Tiger was lurking until the very end. Had fate chosen to nudge a putt or two incrementally toward the cup, the name of Tiger Woods would be engraved on the trophy. But that day will come surely and soon. It is destined to be so.

After having come up a few shots short of winning the 1999 British Open, Tiger patiently sat behind the microphones and answered nearly every question posed to him. He was philosophical in defeat. *"I tried my hardest, I came close, and that's all I can expect of myself."*

Tiger is a 3-D, day-glo, over-amped rock star who
wears his trademark red shirt on the last day of every
tournament, indicating perhaps the bloody aftermath
he anticipates if his game is sharp.

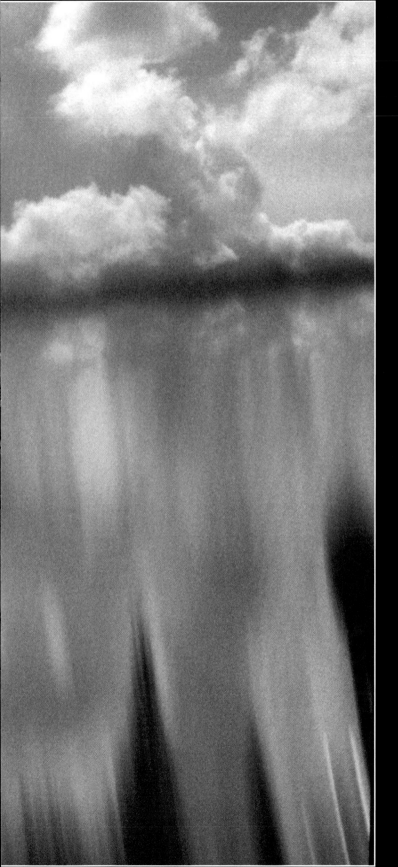

Here is the bottom-line truth: Tiger is a nice, highly intelligent young man with unlimited talent; he has assumed center stage in the global theater where he will remain for the rest of his life. He is one of the most recognizable people on the planet, and his every move bears public scrutiny. His triumphs are magnified, as are his blunders.

As he grows as a person, so will his already enormous popularity. It is almost a certainty that Tiger Woods will be regarded as the greatest golfer of his era, whether or not he ever matches the achievements of the illustrious Golden Bear.